STAND ALONE TRACKS

'70s ROCK

ALLON SAMS

Alfred, the leader in educational publishing, and the National Guitar Workshop, one of America's finest guitar schools, have joined forces to bring you the best, most progressive educational tools possible. We hope you will enjoy this book and encourage you to look for other fine products from Alfred and the National Guitar Workshop.

National Guitar Workshop Book

Approved Curriculum

NATIONAL GUITAR WORKSHOP · Alfred

Acquisition, editorial: Nathaniel Gunod, Workshop Arts
Editorial, music typesetting and internal design: Miriam Davidson, Workshop Arts
Consulting editors: Link Harnsberger, Ron Manus

All songs recorded at Workshop Studios, High Falls, NY
and engineered by Mark Dziuba
The Band: Mark Dziuba, guitar; Allon Sams, piano and organ;
Jerry Rightmer, bass; Gary Denton, drums

Cover photo: Jeff Oshiro
Styling: Martha Widmann • Cover design: Ted Engelbart/Carol Kascsak
Guitar: courtesy of Guitar Center, Hollywood • Model: Joe Roth

All songs composed by Allon A. Sams
Recorded at Stagg Street Studios,
Los Angeles, CA
Engineered by Gary Denton
and Allon Sams
Mixed at Workshop Sounds,
High Falls, NY

TABLE OF CONTENTS

ABOUT THE AUTHOR

Allon A. Sams, keyboardist and studio musician, has worked with David Sanborn, Boney James and Doug Cameron. He is an arranger for Alfred Publishing and has developed MIDI libraries for piano instruction courses. Allon works and lives in Los Angeles.

INTRODUCTION

This *Stand Alone* book and CD focuses on the innovative and experimental sound of rock in the 1970s. The songs are based on either a popular song or group from that era. They are fun to jam with and will challenge both the beginner and the advanced player.

Each song is played by a complete band consisting of drums, bass, rhythm guitar, 2nd guitar and occasionally keyboards. You are the primary soloist. Before playing each tune, listen to it carefully and follow the music to understand the structure. There are no melodies so you can try coming up with your own or just solo in the designated sections. This format for practicing gives you an edge over traditional methods. Not only does it allow you to develop a musical understanding of '70s rock, but it will help you create your own style of playing. If you are a beginner, this method will instantly inspire you to practice more often and you will have fun doing it. If you are a more advance player, this is a great way to keep your chops up.

We all know how hard it can be to get our favorite musician friends together in the same spot at the same time (on time!) to rehearse tunes. With this book and CD you don't have to worry about that. You can practice anytime you wish with the help of your own, real live band! Before you know it, other musicans will be calling *you* to come and play with them. Keep on jammin'!

#1
SOUTHERN HOME
CD Track 2

Southern rock is a unique style that gave bands like Lynard Skynard their signature sound. This tune is similar in feel to a very popualr song made famous by them entitled *Sweet Home Alabama*. Try using G Major Pentatonic and the G Blues scale to solo. Even though this song has only three chords you can make your solo rich and exciting. Start out simply and build in intensity as you play through the tune.

G Major Pentatonic

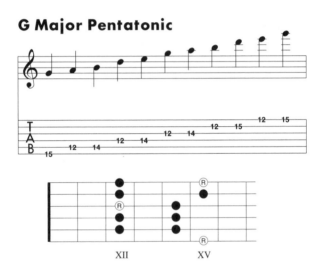

G Blues Scale

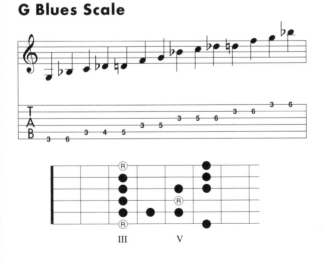

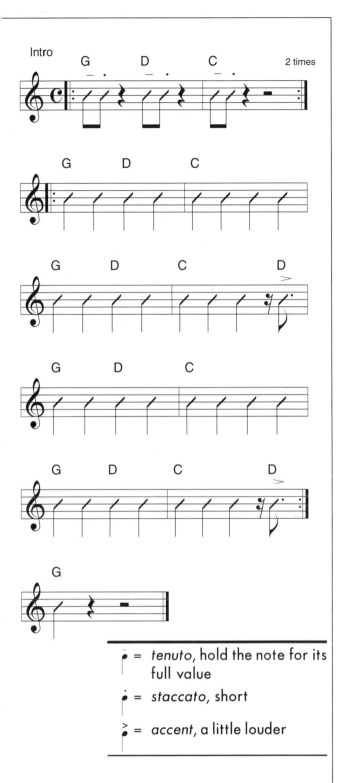

$\bar{\stackrel{\bullet}{}}$ = *tenuto*, hold the note for its full value

$\stackrel{\bullet}{}$ = *staccato*, short

$\stackrel{>}{\bullet}$ = *accent*, a little louder

Form

Four measures of intro. Repeat entire form fourteen times. You play rhythm guitar on choruses* 5, 6, 11 and 12 while 2nd guitar and the piano solo.

*See glossary for explanation of *chorus*

#2
LET'S ROCK
CD Track 3

Led Zeppelin was one of the most famous rock bands of the 70's. The distinct sound of Jimmy Page's guitar coupled with the voice of Robert Plant made its sound unique. This song is derived from one of their most famous tunes, *Rock and Roll*. The structure is similar to a standard blues form. Try using the scales below to help you get ideas for soloing.

A Blues Scale

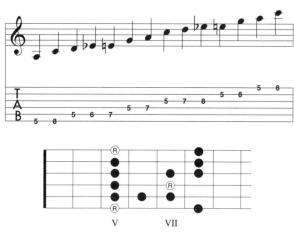

D Blues Scale

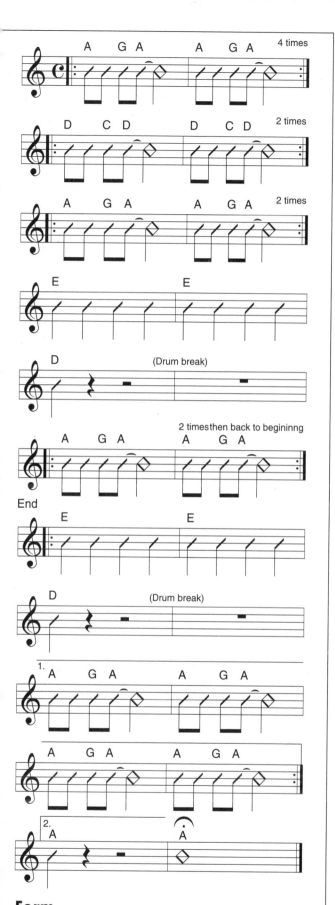

Form

Four measures of drum intro. Repeat entire form eight times. You play rhythm on the third chorus while 2nd guitar solos.

#3
WALK THE WALK
CD Track 4

You will recognize the groove and rhythm in this tune. It is similar a popular song by the band Aerosmith. Unison bass and guitar riffs make this song really rock. Learn the riff first, then use the scales suggested below in your solo. The riff is in the key of E while the rest of the tune is in the key of C.

E Blues Scale

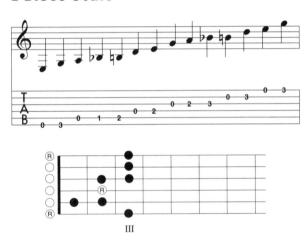

C Major Pentatonic

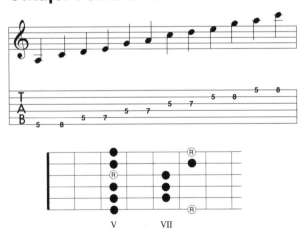

$8vb$ = Play one octave
lower than written

Form

Two measures of drum intro. Repeat entire
form eight times. You play rhythm on choruses
3 and 7 while 2nd guitar solos.

#4
WORK COMES FIRST
CD Track 5

Another popular '70s rock style was *honky-tonk* or *boogie-woogie*. Its characteristic heavy *backbeat* (strong accent on beats two and four) is heard in almost every rock style today. Bachman Turner Overdrive was one of the more popular bands of the time and their tune *Takin' Care of Business* was a big hit. In addition to G and C Major Pentatonic which are shown on pages 6 and 10, try using the B♭ Major Pentatonic and F Major Pentatonic scales.

B♭ Major Pentatonic

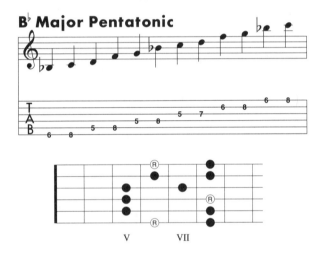

F Major Pentatonic

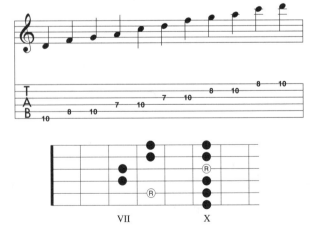

Form

Four measures of drum intro. The A section is played ten times. You solo in choruses 1 through 6, and play rhythm on choruses 7 through 10 while 2nd guitar and piano solo. After the drum and hand-clapping break, you solo over B. After that, you solo through six choruses of the A section then go to the End.

#5
CRUISIN'
CD Track 6

This tune is in the style of a song made famous by the group Foghat (coincidently, they recently recorded in the same studio this CD was recorded in!). A Major Pentatonic will work fine for your solos but you might also want to try the blues version of this scale. When you get to the end, the tempo speeds up gradually, making this song a challenge to solo over.

A Major Pentatonic

A Blues

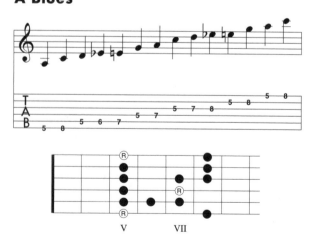

Form

Repeat entire form five times. Fourth time
you play rhythm while 2nd guitar solos.

6

EVERYTHING'S COOL
CD Track 7

The group Free had a big hit called *All Right Now*, which this tune is modeled after. Notice how how the sus4 chords give it a sound all its own. Learn the chords first then listen to the bass line. You will notice that the bass notes are sometimes different from the chord names. This helps to create a nice melodic contrast. Try using the suggested scales combined with your best rock riffs to make your solo fit in the pocket.

A Major Pentatonic

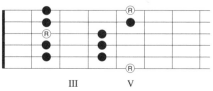

D Major Pentatonic

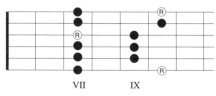

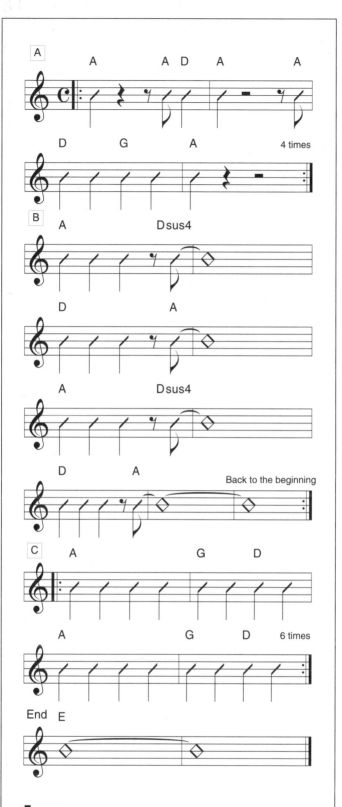

Form

The first two sections, A and B, will be played three times. On the third repetition, you play rhythm guitar while 2nd guitar solos. Then you solo through the C section, and then through two more repetitions of A and B. At the end, the B section is repeated four times while you continue to solo.

#7
OUTLAW
CD Track 8

This next tune is in the style of one made famous by the theatrical rock group Styx. The solid bassline and moving guitar rhythms make this song exciting to solo over. You'll be fine with G Blues Scale, but you should try using D Blues Scale as well. At the end of section C the bands stops briefly—this is where you can start a new solo. The second time around play the *kicks* (accents) with the band.

G Blues Scale

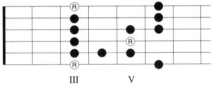

III   V

D Blues Scale

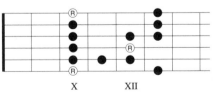

X   XII

Form

Repeat entire form five times. Play rhythm while 2nd guitar solos in the second D section.

#8
SWEET LOVIN'
CD Track 9

The '70s wouldn't be complete without the Rolling Stones. Keith Richards set the musical foundation for this supergroup and his style of playing has influenced guitarists worldwide. This song, in the style of *Brown Sugar,* should give you plenty of room to try out some cool licks. Have fun with this one!

D Major Pentatonic

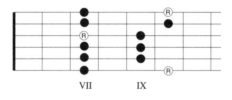

G Major Pentatonic

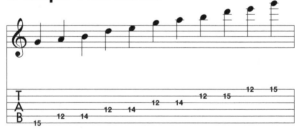

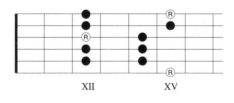

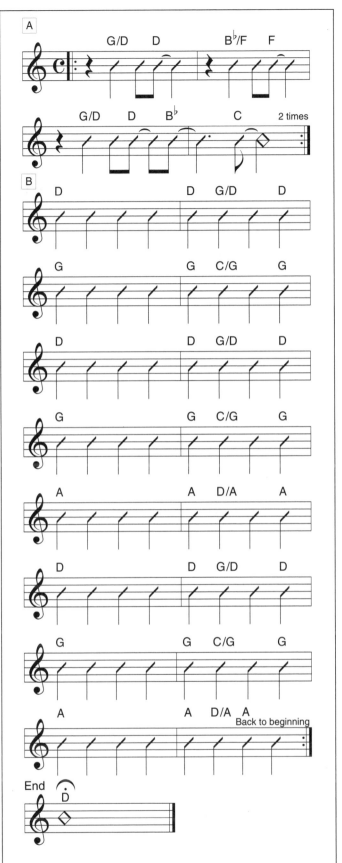

Form

Repeat entire form six times. Third time through you play rhythm while 2nd guitar solos over the B section. *Vamp* (repeat) on the A section six times while you solo to the end.

#9
FEELING FINE
CD Track [10]

Humble Pie was an influential band for guitarists in the '70s. This song is based on *I Don't Need No Doctor* and gives you an example of just how powerful this group was. The E and A Blues Scales work well over these chord changes. Listen to and learn the rhythm guitar patterns in section [A] before you start.

E Blues Scale

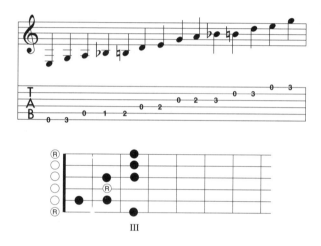

A Blues Scale

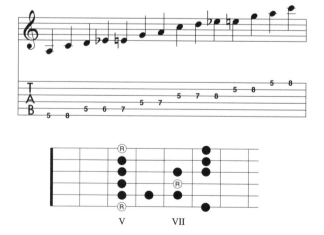

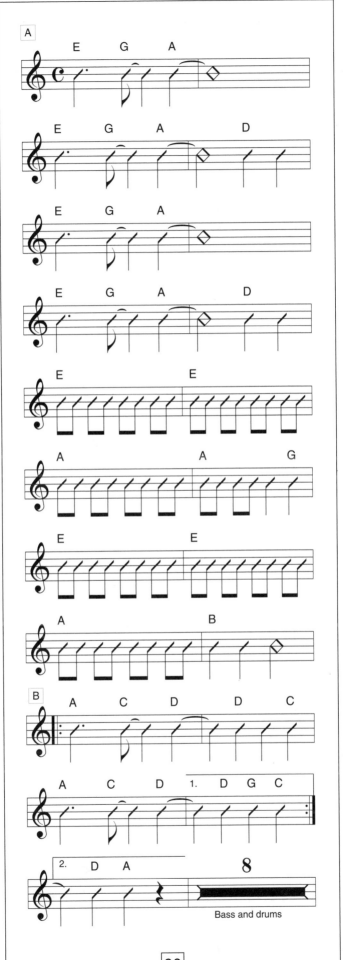

Bass and drums

23

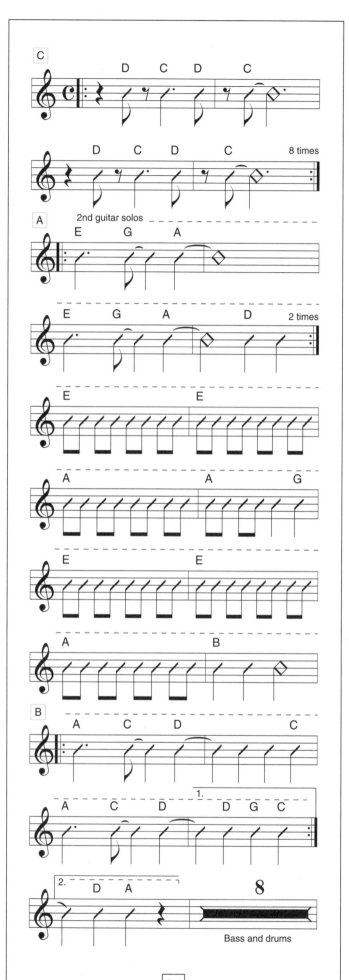

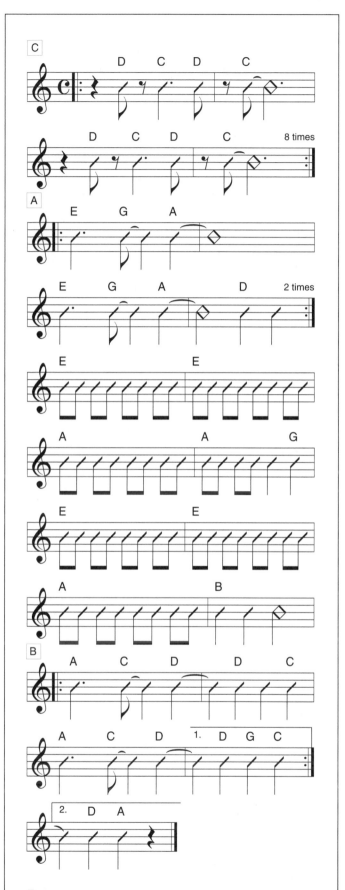

Form

Entire form happens three times. Second time through you play rhythm while 2nd guitar solos.

#10
JAM THE BLUES
CD Track 11

The Allman Brothers Band brought the blues
into their rock and roll by combining soulful
rock vocals with screaming slide guitar solos. Listen to the other instruments while you
are playing rhythm. During the kicks, keep
soloing right into the next section. Use the D
Blues scale and if you have a slide, now's the
time to put it to use!

D Blues Scale

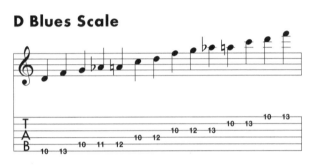

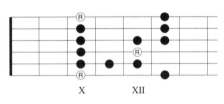

X   XII

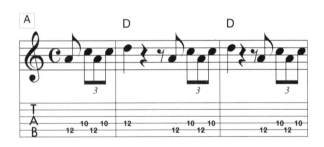

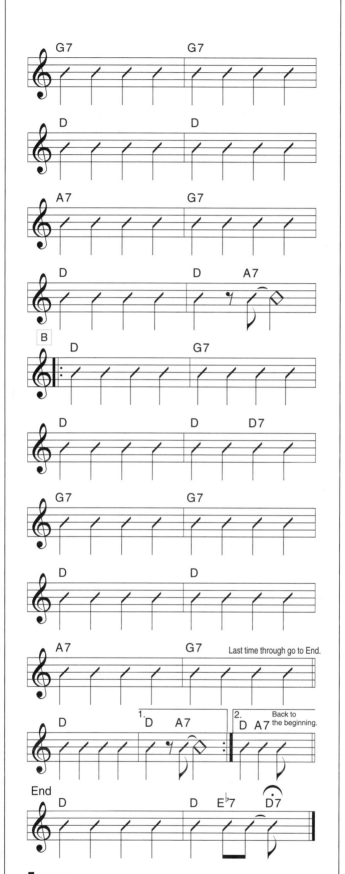

Form

Repeat entire form five times. Third time through you play rhythm while 2nd guitar solos.

APPENDIX
ADDITONAL SCALES

Here are a few more scales you can use in your solos. Try experimenting and use your imagination.

D Minor Pentatonic

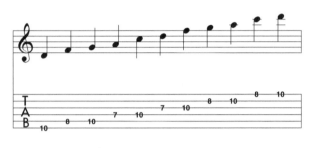

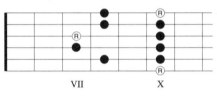

C# Phrygian

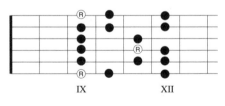

Blues scales can be used in many styles of music ranging from country to rock and roll. Here is the blues scale in three different keys.

C Blues Scale

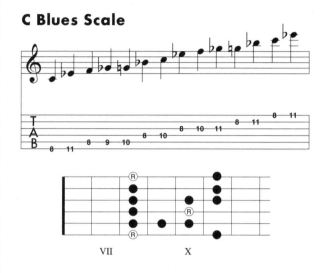

F Blues Scale

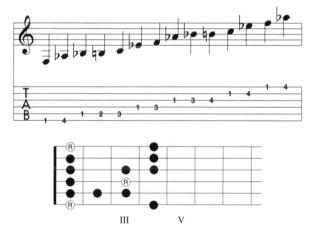

B Blues Scale

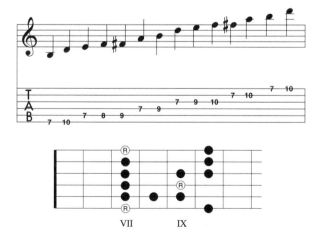

GLOSSARY

Chorus: Usually the main theme or *hook* section of a song. It is the part that you usually remember best. Musicians often use this term to refer to the entire song played one time through, which is how it is used in this book.

Kick: This is commonly known as a rhythmic accent. Usually the rhythm section of the band plays it, but it can also include the melody instrument or the singer.

Lick: A short, self-contianed musical idea which can be used in many different contexts. Some licks can be used in various styles. A country lick may work well in a blues tune while a jazz lick may not work well in a rock song.

Riff: A re-occuring melodic line that is usually integral to the rhythm of a tune.

Unison: When two or more instruments are playing exactly the same notes or melody at the same time.

Vamp: To continue repeating a certain section of music until cued to stop. This often happens at the end of a song. When you hear a recording fade out, this is almost always a vamp on the chorus.

DISCOGRAPHY

Some of the groups and artists that helped shape the sound of rock music in the '70s are listed below.

Aerosmith
The Allman Brothers Band
Bachman Turner Overdrive
The Band
Jeff Beck
Blind Faith
Blood, Sweat and Tears
Boston
Eric Clapton
Creedence Clearwater Revival
Derek and the Dominoes
The Eagles
Emerson, Lake and Palmer
Foghat
Peter Frampton
Free
Frigid Pink
Humble Pie
Nils Lofgren
Lynard Skynard
The Moody Blues
Pink Floyd
Santana
Rod Stewart
The Rolling Stones
Styx
Traffic
Uriah Heep
The Who
Yes
Led Zeppelin